To See, To Feel, To Know:
Experiencing the Holocaust Through the Virginia Holocaust Museum

By

Elisabeth Anne Custalow

THE
Donning Company
Publishers

THE DONNING COMPANY PUBLISHERS
184 BUSINESS PARK DRIVE, SUITE 206
VIRGINIA BEACH, VIRGINIA 23462-6533

STEVE MULL, GENERAL MANAGER
BARBARA BUCHANAN, OFFICE MANAGER
KATHLEEN SHERIDAN, SENIOR EDITOR
STEPHANIE DANKO, GRAPHIC DESIGNER
MARY ELLEN WHEELER, PROOFREADER
LYNN PARROTT, IMAGING SPECIALIST
SCOTT RULE, DIRECTOR OF MARKETING
TRAVIS GALLUP, MARKETING COORDINATOR

DENNIS WALTON, PROJECT DIRECTOR

Library of Congress Cataloging-in-Publication Data

Custalow, Elisabeth Anne.
  To see, to feel, to know : experiencing the Holocaust through the Virginia Holocaust Museum / by Elisabeth Anne Custalow.
      p. cm.
  Includes bibliographical references and index.
  ISBN 1-57864-305-8 (alk. paper)
  1. Virginia Holocaust Museum (Richmond, Va.) 2. Holocaust, Jewish (1939-1945)--Museums--Virginia--Richmond. 3. Holocaust memorials--Virginia--Richmond. I. Title.
  D804.175.R53C87 2005
  940.53'18'07475523--dc22
                                          2005002441

Printed in the United States of America by Walsworth Publishing Company

Dedicated to the more than six million human beings, including 1.5 million children, who lost their lives during the Holocaust.

TABLE**OF**CONTENTS

ERIC CANTOR

CHIEF DEPUTY MAJORITY WHIP
MEMBER OF CONGRESS
7TH DISTRICT, VIRGINIA

Dear Visitor:

Richmond is a city with a deep history. The city's landscape is peppered with historical markers and monuments that bear silent witness to Richmond's long and complex history. History, however, is not just a moment--but a ripple that pulses through time and touches everyone--making us all members of events that happened before we were born.

Most of the markers and monuments here in Richmond are based on local events that shaped the city over the last 400 years. Richmonders, however, also recognize the dramatic world events that shaped Richmond from afar.

The Virginia Holocaust Museum's location in Richmond's oldest neighborhood fuses Richmond's past with the World's past. The museum's exhibits engage visitors to experience and understand the horror of the Holocaust--a history that belongs to all of us. The presence of the Holocaust Museum in Richmond serves as an important reminder to all of us that world events influence and change us every day. This museum offers us a vivid challenge to positively contribute to our community and our world everyday.

Sincerely,

Eric Cantor
Member of Congress

olocaust. To some, the word is one with no impact and is simply associated with others from history: Hitler and World War II. Others can say nothing about the term except that it is a part of the past.

But to others it is a word as familiar as their own names and can no more be separated from memory than can smoke from flame.

Holocaust. Only one word for the more than six million slaughtered and millions more scarred. Only one word for a period of five years that, in effect, did last and has lasted far longer. And to billions of human beings who have lived since 1945, it is just one word. Only a word.

Museum visitors pass by cobblestones from the Warsaw ghetto and rails from Treblinka death camp when entering through cracked glass doors symbolizing the Night of Broken Glass

But that one word has a scope to stretch from Austria to Italy and from Auschwitz to Treblinka. That one word is spread across bloodied forest fields. That one word has walked countless death marches and rumbled over hundreds of miles of train tracks. That one word is suspended in chambers of experimentation performed on human beings, and it resides in ravines dug by the men whose bodies would fill them. That one word is the walls of underground rooms made of dirt and the floor of attic crawlspaces where families sought protection. That one word is the skin-draped skeleton of a survivor and the naked body of a nursing mother left now to feed vultures. That one word is the fist of evil and malice, and its opposition is the will to live when every earthly power strives to make it impossible. That one word is the contempt that breeds hatred, and its opponent is the miracle of enduring.

Holocaust. Each letter is composed of millions of stories, more than can ever be heard and too few to explain what that one word really means.

There are stories that are too heavy for the tongue to lift the syllables, and stories that were silenced before they

Portraits of Virginia Holocaust Museum major contributors, the Carol and Marcus Weinstein Family and the Sonny and Jay Weinberg Family, hang in the reception area.

Visitors begin their journey by following the train tracks.

could be spoken. And there are stories that are waiting, ready for the ears of those willing to learn how to pronounce one word. To know that a single word is written in volumes.

In 1997, the Virginia Holocaust Museum opened in a former school building of Richmond's Temple Beth El. By 2000, the museum had grown too large for the five rooms of that location, and the Virginia legislature offered a former tobacco warehouse in historic Shockoe Bottom. Work began on the building in 2002, and the museum is now open to the public at 2000 East Cary Street.

Jay M. Ipson, Mark Fetter, and L. Al Rosenbaum founded the museum with the goal of tolerance through education. The museum's mission statement is four-part:

- To remember the victims and heroes who lived through or perished during the Holocaust;

- To combat intolerance, anti-Semitism, prejudice and hate;

- To provide educational materials in the Holocaust Education Resource Center;

- To increase awareness and understanding of the Holocaust in the general community.

It was decided that the museum would tell the story of Jay Ipson's family, who were Holocaust survivors, by guiding visitors in an experience of authentic re-creation. The museum's symbol, which Al Rosenbaum designed, speaks of that pervading purpose. The museum describes it as follows:

> *The symbol for the Virginia Holocaust Museum is a menorah surrounded by barbed wire. The six-armed candelabrum illustrates the story of the Holocaust, while the barbed wire symbolizes imprisonment. The broken Star of David stands for all the lives and Jewish families that were torn apart in the Holocaust. The six candles memorialize the 6 million Jews who perished at the hands of the Nazis. The short candle honors the 1.5 million Jewish children who died. The red paint represents the bloodshed; the blue symbolizes hope.*

The museum has chosen to educate visitors through an internal experience more than an external one. The visitor experiences it with the gut, nerves, heart—everything that is normally kept shielded from the process of learning. The eyes—to read what text is posted on the walls and to see all the details of a ghetto or a shop with broken windows—are but the means for the information to travel to all the places where it will truly be registered and understood. If you jump at a sound in a distant room or hear your heartbeat as you crawl through the tunnel, it is simply your body beginning to feel the impact of the Holocaust on a human life, something the brain alone is not able to do.

Sometimes we have not been taught to speak a word that is not a part of the language of our minds and memories, and to use each of our senses to complete its meaning. And so our concept of what happened decades ago across an ocean is without color, voice, odor, taste, and a feeling in our bones and muscles. But at the Virginia Holocaust Museum you feel it is happening in your very presence at this very moment. You feel like a prisoner and you feel like a survivor, and at that moment you know what six million means. It is one plus one plus one plus one…

The museum's menorah symbol is depicted on the outside of the building as well as inside.

CHAPTER ONE

REIGN OF HATRED: THE NAZIS' ASCENT

Where does the story of the Holocaust begin? With the end of World War I, with Hitler's ascension to power, with the murder of the first person called Jew? No date one chooses can carry the full burden of the beginning of the worst genocide in human history. Any action undertaken is only the completion of a picture that one has been drawing, systematically or sketchily, for months, years, or a lifetime.

Prejudice against the Jewish people did not spring into being in the early twentieth century. During the Middle Ages and other periods, Jews were the subject of antipathy and persecution in European countries. The beast of racism lay dormant at times before savagely striking out, and it revealed its full, unrelenting, and unfathomable ferocity from 1939 to 1945.

Anti-Semitism was an undercurrent of the mentality of much of Europe at the end of World War I. Those living on the land at that time had inherited views held by previous generations. Jews were often considered conspiratorial outsiders and a dark, subhuman plague on society. Although the majority of the German populace did not proclaim the degree of anti-Jewish sentiment espoused by Adolf Hitler, his stance would certainly not be something to dissuade many from supporting him.

Hitler's political career was sparked when he joined the German Workers' Party, which, shortly thereafter, he named the National Socialist German Workers' Party, and by July 1921 he was its chairman. The Nazi party, consistently anti-Semitic, seemed on the verge of failure for several years, but in 1933 Hitler became Germany's chan-

Nazis' attempts to destroy Jewish culture resulted in bonfires fueled by books written by Jews or about Jews.

cellor under President Paul von Hindenburg and established the authority of the SS (protection squads or "Blackshirts") and SA (stormtroopers or "Brownshirts") forces. The Nazi party would project itself as the solution to Germany's economic troubles while clinging to Hitler's own desire to "cure" Germany of the "parasitic Jew." Hitler used the concept of social Darwinism to support his prejudice by claiming that the Aryans or Germans were the purest of races, with such groups as Jews being a dangerous inferiority. The Enabling Act, passed in 1933, empowered the Nazis to enact laws without the accordance of parliament. This measure would place total authority in their hands.

When von Hindenburg died in 1934, Hitler named himself *führer*, "leader," and initiated his dictatorship. He answered to no one. He was subject to no one. He believed there was no one to whom he must give an account, and he acted unblinkingly on that belief in his own supremacy. He possessed the authority of government and the power of the military, and he committed to the completion of his consuming goal: the removal—the eradication—of the Jewish people.

The movement of history toward the murder of millions of Jews did not come in a single, swift stroke following Hitler's rise to power. The degradation of a people came in state-sanctioned stages.

Before there were flames in the ovens of crematoriums, there were flames of a different sort to rob a man of his intellectual achievements. Any book with a Jewish author or publisher or that treated a Jewish theme in a tone that did not condemn it was burned.

The livelihood of the Jews, who were often considered inordinately wealthy, was a perpetual target. The Nazis led a boycott, positioning stormtroopers with inflammatory

Hitler proclaims protection for Christian religions but will punish preachers who speak out against Nazism.

Restrictive laws told Jews what they were forbidden to do.

Restrictions were meant to make life difficult for Jews in hopes that they would emigrate elsewhere.

signs outside Jewish stores and businesses. Sometimes anti-Semitic sayings disgraced the windows of shops, and Jewish businessmen faced harassment from Nazi mouths and, sometimes, their fists or boots.

The doors to employment and education were slammed in the face of the Jewish population. They were prohibited from maintaining civil service positions or serving as doctors, dentists, judges, or lawyers; and they could seek an education for their children in Jewish schools only. The small pleasures of life as a member of a community and a citizen of a country were no longer available to them. No swimming in public pools, no stroll through a public park, no playing on a public playground. It became impossible for someone with Jewish blood to inherit a farm or to serve in Germany's military, an affront to everyone who still felt patriotic, especially to the men who had been decorated for bravery during the First World War.

In September 1935, the Nuremberg Laws were passed with two objectives: to nullify Jewish citizenship and to declare it illegal for a Jew and a German to marry or engage in a sexual relationship.

Hitler's Nazis had already attacked and picked clean the freedoms of Germany's Jewish citizens, though Jews could no longer be called "citizens." They were treated the way they were viewed: as something less than. But the economic deprivation, legal impotence, and personal humiliation of Jewish men, women, and children were not sufficient to satisfy Hitler's malevolence. He would not stop until he had achieved an outcome absolute, inescapable, and final.

The passing of these legal measures, combined with the indifference on the part of many German citizens, would figuratively fuel the trains that would transport Jews toward the fulfillment of Hitler's diabolical undertaking.

CHAPTER TWO

Forced from Home: The Train Station

You arrive at the train station. You have come this way on a forced march or on a truck or a wagon or a bus filled with others so very different from you. Some have the bald scalp of an old man; some have the baldness of a baby. There are former teachers here with former students. There are those who were once rich and those who were always penniless. There are girls once called giddy and girls whose shyness has become their shield. There are boys who could have been doctors and men who once were.

And you are here, too, with your talents and your memories and your love and your old wishes and your beautiful, dusty picture of what life would look like and your satchel of sheets, two blankets, heavy shoes, and warm clothing and no sharp objects. And all around you, everyone holds a satchel filled with the same items as yours. Everyone is so different from you. But you are the same in the one way that matters. You are a Jew.

You boarded your wagon with the barrel of a guard's gun just inches away. The guards have no patience for the old, whose knees do not know the guard is in a hurry, or for the mother holding the hand of her child to help him up the steps.

You have been jostled and jarred for miles now as you stand on a wagon that shows no sympathy to its tight pack of human cargo. How many miles it has been you do not know or how many are left. You clutch your satchel and wait. You apologize to your neighbor and caress your elbow when a bump bangs it against his.

Finally at the train station, you are loaded onto one of many cattle cars that will roll across the Reichsbahn, Germany's railway. You will travel through scenery you have

At the museum's Dachau/Buchenwald exhibit, visitors queue up on the train station platform to begin their journey.

Families, struggling to stay together, are told "resettling in the East" will improve their situation.

Museum 3-D model with the Wall of Honor that acknowledges those who help the museum fulfill its mission.

never before passed by, but you will not see it now either. For days you will stand in a cattle car packed with eighty to one hundred other passengers. There is only a bucket for a toilet, and it quickly overflows. Outside the air is clean, but inside human beings die, are mourned and rot, dead from a lack of air, water, and food. The sun does not illuminate a space surrounded by steel, and you have no rest for your feet, no escape from the stench of urine and human decomposition.

In many cases, you have paid for the privilege of taking a ride. Often, Jews were told they were being resettled or moved to a location where employment was attainable, and they were charged a fee for transportation.

When the train comes to a halt, the deportees, who have already turned in all valuables, including house keys, before leaving on this journey, are made to hand over their satchels. The contents will be given to German citizens. The deportees will wear a thin camp uniform of poor cotton. Some passengers are sent to concentration camps to perform hard labor. Others are sent to death camps to be gassed.

The train station is the first stage of your visit to the Virginia Holocaust Museum. The deportation mural shows the faces of men, women, and children, representing millions who are so very different and just the same.

Founders sculpture was designed by Al Rosenbaum and manufactured by Andy C. Jackson.

CHAPTER THREE

Slow Murder: The Concentration Camps of Dachau and Buchenwald

The Virginia Holocaust Museum has deposited you at Dachau/Buchenwald, and you must enter through a gate inscribed with "Jedem Das Seine." This slogan, meaning "To each what he deserves," was posted at Buchenwald. New arrivals at Dachau were greeted with the ironical words "Arbeit Macht Frei": "Work will set you free."

You have stepped inside the barracks for a group of prisoners, inside a semblance of the conditions in which men and women were made to reside. Their furnishings were tiered bunks crammed with ten times the number of bodies they could support, perhaps a straw mattress to sleep and eat on, no pillow and not enough blankets by half to keep away the chill that might claim a life. Lice and bedbugs spread rapidly in such tight quarters, where sanitation was forbidden.

To even enter the barracks, the deportees had to survive the first selection. Upon each train's arrival at a camp, the young, the old, and the ill were killed— shot or gassed before they really knew where they had come. Those who were chosen to remain at the camp, for an uncertain period of time, were dehumanized and treated as creatures with no identity beyond "prisoner." The characteristics that differentiated one appearance from another were abolished. Men's beards were shaved. The head of each prisoner was shaved, and the strands of hair might be

Nazis deemed it necessary to bind their mocking philosophy, "To each what he deserves," in ironwork.

used to make socks for submariners.

All prisoners were forced to disrobe, including women who suffered the humiliation of compulsory stripping before men. In exchange for their usable clothes, the prisoners received insufficient clothing that fit sizes other than their own.

Human beings then had no names. They had numbers, sometimes tattooed on their skin with crude instruments that caused severe pain, bleeding, and swelling.

A triangular patch of varying color was the one distinction made between individuals. It explained why the Nazis deemed each worthy of the harshest cruelty that could be methodically crafted.

Nazis in camps would torture prisoners for information or for malice.

The categories of prisoners are as follows:

AMERICAN POWs—*JEWISH-AMERICAN SOLDIERS* were sometimes interned in concentration camps, such as Berga, rather than POW camps.

YELLOW PATCHES—*JEWISH PRISONERS*

BLUE—*EMIGRANTS*

BROWN—*GYPSIES*

RED—*POLITICAL PRISONERS*

BLACK—*ASOCIALS*

GREEN—*HABITUAL CRIMINALS*

PINK—*HOMOSEXUALS*

PURPLE—*JEHOVAH'S WITNESSES*

The men who look out from the barracks of the Virginia Holocaust Museum wear patches that signify a cross-section of the camps' population of prisoners. Their heads and beards are shaved, and they wear the identical camp uniform. But their faces are not identical. Each looks out with his own eyes. They are not the same, nor could they be. Even though the goal of the guards was to remove all traces of individualism, identity, and human characteristics, there remained some piece of each man, each woman to show that a soul cannot be shaved away.

The men in these barracks represent the more than 80,000 human beings who lost their lives at Dachau and Buchenwald. The loss is a fraction of the deaths that occurred at thousands of camps spread across Germany and German-occupied territories. By May 1945, more than 9,000 camps had been in operation, including six death camps in Poland. Dachau, the first concentration camp, was established in 1933 but was the destination mainly for political prisoners in its early years.

Life at the camps was designed to fulfill the unambiguous goal of starving and working the prisoners to death. The tightly controlled rations were meager: maybe for the day a drink called coffee, a bowl of broth, and a piece of dry bread. So deficient were the meals that prisoners were willing to risk execution to find a few blades of grass or some rotting garbage to eat.

The starvation diet was incapable of providing the type of energy and stamina needed to perform the hard labor required of the prisoners. The guards ordered the demanding tasks of digging ditches, chopping wood, felling trees, rock quarrying, and building roads and structures with the intention of full and final exhaustion and death from overwork. The instruction to carry heavy rocks across a field and back again—at a run—could be delivered with no result necessary other than the wearing down of the human body. To stop and rest for only one second was punishable by whip or club. Even a man or woman working steadily might be beaten or killed solely for the guards' enjoyment. The guards inflicted other beatings during interrogations as a way to gain information about resistance fighters. Many prisoners died as a result.

The prisoners—both men and women—worked long days with little sleep. A large part of their daily "free time"

Prisoners in the men's barracks needed to secure their soup bowls for the watery sustenance that was doled out at mealtime.

was spent standing outdoors for roll call. No matter the weather—an extreme of heat or cold, torrents of rain—roll call took place, and it took hours. Some men, their bodies critically weakened and their health faltering, died during the torture, which could last almost twenty hours. Others froze to death. But even the dead and the dying were counted.

The spare meals, excruciating physical labor, and exposure to the elements did nothing to strengthen the prisoners against the camps' rampant diseases. In the close and unsanitary confines of the bunks, disease was practically inevitable, and the camps lacked proper medical equipment and care. The ill were considered weak and useless and were threatened by the likelihood of going to the gas chamber before the disease had a chance to take their lives. The "healthy" could be sent to the gas chambers, too, however, if room was needed to accommodate new arrivals.

The medical supplies and procedures at the camps may have been deplorable, but protecting the health of the German military was of highest importance to the men in charge of the camps. The prisoners were frequently subjected to painful exper-iments, two of which have been re-created in the museum's Dachau/Buchenwald room. Each was performed to aid the German Air Force, known as the Luftwaffe. One reproduction shows a low-pressure experiment imposed on a prisoner suspended in an airtight booth with no oxy-gen mask. The other experiment was conducted to see how long a human being would be able to survive in freezing water. Sun lamps and boiling water would be employed to find the best method for raising body temperature.

The prisoners in the barracks are not able to leave, although visitors can come and go. The prisoners are depictions and cannot speak in language interpreted by the ear. Their presence, though, tells the story of men who were tested to the limits of human endurance. They have met evil embodied in ordinary men and women, and they are aware that such evil can spring up again in bodies not belonging to Nazis.

Prisoners endured cruel "scientific experiments," providing statistical infor-mation to enhance the Luftwaffe.

CHAPTER FOUR

SUPPLYING THE NEED
HYDE FARMLANDS

Dr. Curt Bondy knew times were hard and were not going to get easier. Opportunities for Jews were being squeezed out like the last few drops of water in a sponge. The forceful unemployment of Jewish members of the legal, medical, and educational professions burdened the professional class. The youths would be next; restricting their education was a part of Nazi policy.

So in the late 1930s prior to Kristallnacht, Dr. Bondy, a German-Jewish professor, arranged for Jews between fifteen and twenty-five years of age to acquire hands-on agricultural experience. At a farm in Gross-Breesen, Germany, the participants learned to raise livestock, care for crops, and mend clothing. His goal was to endow them with skills to enable them to emigrate. Out of 200 students, 150 did emigrate from Germany.

The Virginia Holocaust Museum portrays the opportunity granted to the thirty-six immigrants to Hyde Farmlands in Burkeville, Virginia. Cousins William B. Thalhimer Sr., owner of Thalhimer's Department Store, and Morton G. Thalhimer Sr., real estate financier, bought the 1,600-acre farm to give the young people in Bondy's program a place to go. While raising chickens and tobacco, the students received shares in the farm. Many of the young men joined America's armed forces when the nation entered World War II in 1941.

With America's entrance into the war, the program at Hyde Farmlands was discontinued. The students, however, now decades older, gather annually to honor friendships formed and to recall the time in their lives when a

The house at Hyde Farmlands still stands as testimony to Virginia's role in the history of the Holocaust.

CHAPTER FIVE

THE NIGHT OF BROKEN GLASS: KRISTALLNACHT

The quiet of sleep is shattered. A cacophony of destruction awakens Jews to a conscious nightmare. Jewish shops and homes are being ransacked. Someone is hurling the merchandise of stores and warehouses and the furniture, appliances, and other belongings in homes through windows and torching them in the streets. SA mobs, other Nazis, and the brutes who will join any violent endeavor spend fifteen hours pillaging Jewish residential areas and setting them aflame. German firefighters use their hoses to save non-Jewish buildings only. Synagogues—houses of reverent worship—are not spared, nor are the scrolls they contain. Frankfurt, Germany's Boernplatz Synagogue, depicted at the Virginia Holocaust Museum, is one casualty. Jewish cemeteries are desecrated. Jewish men, women, and children are attacked on the streets or pulled from their homes, beaten, and killed.

Radios, such as the one at the museum, broadcast this announcement, whose official tone is as frightening as the din of breaking glass, buildings crumbling in flames, and the screams of terror and pain:

Achtung Juden! Mit sofortiger Wirkung verboten: Besuch von öffentlichen Schulen; arbeiten in öffentlichen Bueros; benutzung des Bürgersteigs; der gelbe Davidstern muss immer auf der Brust und auf dem Rücken getragen warden. Zuwiderhandlungen werden mit Verhaftungen bestraft.

Attention Jews! With immediate attention forbidden: Attending public schools, working in public offices, using sidewalks; the yellow Star of David has got to be worn on the chest and on the back at all times. Contraventions will be punished with imprisonment.

The Nazis looted and destroyed Jewish-owned or -operated businesses.

An 1850 torah scroll from Prague survived the Holocaust.

You are on the streets of Germany during Kristallnacht, "The Night of Broken Glass." The Virginia Holocaust Museum has re-created the night of November 9–10, 1938. The reproduction of the F. W. Woolworth Company store in Berlin, an American business owned by Christians, shows the ruin that was created in one night. The store was selected for destruction because Jews managed it. The graffiti on its broken windows tells Germans, "Deutsche! Wehrt Euch! Kauft nicht bei Juden!," an injunction not to patronize Jewish shops, and threatens, "Weckwaschung, Urlaub in Buchenwald," that a vacation in Buchenwald will be the consequence for cleaning up the graffiti-stained stores.

Days before the demolition occurred, on November 7, seventeen-year-old Jewish student Herschel Grynszpan had entered the German Embassy in Paris and shot Ernst vom Rath, German third secretary. The teenager was infuriated by the treatment of his parents, who were among several thousand Polish-Jewish residents of Germany forced from that country to the border of Poland, where they were refused entry. They had no choice but to form a camp for themselves at the border in crude conditions.

Nazi propaganda described Kristallnacht as the German population's spontaneous reaction to the assassination of vom Rath. In reality, members of the Nazi

leadership had long been planning an extensive attack against the Jews, and vom Rath's death was the excuse for which they had been waiting. The violence resulted in the destruction of thousands of businesses and synagogues and the deaths of ninety-one Jews. Many more were seriously wounded, and 30,000 Jewish men would soon be sent to concentration camps.

To punish the Jews further for the death of vom Rath and inciting such indignation, a fine was ordered of 1 billion reichsmarks. For a people who had lost their homes, their businesses, and their economic opportunities, that amount, equal in 1938 to $400 million, was impracticable. They bore the cost of the repairs, too, because their insurance payments were seized.

The Kristallnacht scene at the museum includes a unique doll made by Kathe Kruse. Anna Fisher bought the doll for her daughter, Eva, in 1933 in Germany. Information concerning Germany's payment of portions of taxes to the state's churches is posted on a wall in the museum's Kristallnacht room. The speech from which excerpts are taken asserts that no person had or would face religious persecution in

Homes were invaded and ransacked, leaving families shocked and terrified.
Inset: The manufacturer of Kathe Kruse dolls was put out of business when Jewish distributors were prohibited from working.

This artistic representation of the Shoah, by L. Al Rosenbaum, depicts events from 1938 to 1945.

Crates sent to Herman and Tosia Joel of Virginia by a cousin in Germany in anticipation of their arrival in the U.S. The crates were never collected.

Germany and that no influence of beliefs or banning of the practice of religious acts had ever occurred. It was declared, however, that the state would discipline ministers who denigrated the state, its actions, or its rulers.

In the early hours of November 10, the shroud of smoke and its pungency linger in the air. The sun's new rays are reflected on the millions and millions of shards of glass that litter the streets and sidewalks and are crunched underfoot. The glare off the jagged pieces is bright and painful, but it cannot be blinding.

CHAPTER SIX

ALMOST FREE: THE SS *ST. LOUIS*

Devastated financially and emotionally by the deadly and destructive rage aimed at them during Kristallnacht, many of Germany's Jewish residents sought to escape the perils of that country for safety elsewhere. High numbers of Jews attempted to emigrate until the start of World War II in 1939 eliminated that possibility.

The SS *St. Louis*, a German ocean liner, departed from Hamburg Dock for Cuba in May 1939 with the intention that its 937 passengers, more than 900 of whom were Jews, would not return to Europe. The ship pulled into the port of Havana on May 27. Although the passengers had paid their fare and possessed visas that should have allowed them to enter Cuba, the country permitted only twenty-eight to do so.

The remaining passengers sailed to Florida and into waters patrolled by the U.S. Coast Guard. The ship's captain, Gustav Schroeder, and a passenger committee requested help from the United States, but none was given. While the Coast Guard stayed close to prevent anyone from jumping and swimming to shore, the passengers solicited the aid of President Franklin Roosevelt via telegram. On June 5, they were informed they would not be allowed to dock.

The ship turned back toward Europe on June 6. Belgium, England, France, and the Netherlands permitted entry into their nations, but within months Nazi-ruled Germany would eventually fold much of western Europe into its domain. The only passengers of the *St. Louis* to avoid the Holocaust were among those admitted into England. The other two-thirds were victims of the very ruthlessness they had almost escaped.

The *St. Louis* was the last ship allowed to sail from Nazi Germany carrying Jewish refugees.

American anti-immigration and anti-Semitic attitudes played a role in keeping the SS *St. Louis* off the Miami coast.

At the Virginia Holocaust Museum, the SS *St. Louis* continues to bob in free waters, waiting for the words that will determine the fate of the families on board. Days earlier, men and women and boys and girls had celebrated their imminent arrival on soil not pounded by Nazi boots. They now anxiously waited near the coast of the United States for the American government's response.

The murals at the museum show the cities of Havana and Miami, which had held—and denied—the lure of freedom. Rejected by the governments of two countries an ocean away from Nazi policy, the passengers of the *St. Louis* would cross that ocean once more but in an atmosphere much different from the first. Their Nazi captors would use this experience to further their own anti-Semitic goals. Cuba and the United States of America had turned the Jews away, and in Nazi rhetoric, this proved that no nation, no people, and no land wanted them.

CHAPTER SEVEN

CAGED:
KOVNO GHETTO

History's cycle of anti-Semitism saw the return of the Middle Ages, when ghettos were produced again in European nations during the twentieth century. The Jews who were enclosed faced overcrowding, starvation served to them by the Nazis' rations, horrible health, and disconnection from every other area of the city and from the normalcy they had previously enjoyed. Confined like criminals, the families inside the ghettos were made to wear a yellow Star of David so that there could be no question as to their identity. An attempt to flee the ghetto brought a quick bullet from a guard's ready gun. The number of dead—from starvation, disease, and execution—rose steadily, and the increase was evident as the bodies were often left in the street.

Jay Ipson, one of the youngest Holocaust survivors in Richmond, witnessed and experienced ghetto subsistence personally. He lived in Kovno Ghetto with his parents, Israel and Edna Ipson, formerly Ipp, and Edna's parents.

The story of the Ipsons, a Lithuanian-Jewish family, is depicted at the museum in the spaces Kovno Ghetto through the Hiding Place. Nazi forces invaded the family's hometown of Kovno, the capital of Lithuania, on June 24, 1941, when Jay was six years old. By the end of the occupation, Nazis and Lithuanians who had been neighbors of the victims would kill more than 90 percent of the Jews in Lithuania.

As you stand in Kovno Ghetto, the fear, discomfort, and despair are as clear as the barbed wire that surrounds it.

The Nazis cordoned off sections of a village using wire, brick, board, or stone fencing. These cobblestones had formed the pavement within the Warsaw Ghetto.

Guards selected Jews as ghetto policemen to maintain order and see that Nazi procedures were followed.

Mouth of a well led to hiding places within the ghetto. Sides of the well also hid valuables of inhabitants.

Weekly per person rations: 2 ounces of salt, 3 ounces of grain, 4 ounces of flour, 4 ounces of meat, 2 slices of bread, a handful of vegetables, and, for workers only, 3/4 ounce lard.

Female laborers shovel coal onto trains for German use.

Nieh Shul was the heart of Jewish life.

Most of the Jews' possessions were taken upon entrance to the ghetto, and Nazis and Lithuanians would be the recipients. Living in houses that lacked indoor plumbing, the ghetto residents carried water home from the well and used out-houses. The sanitation in ghettos was poor, and lice were abundant.

Sickness and starvation were pre-scribed for the Jewish people the way medicine and correct care would be distributed to someone living in dif-ferent circumstances. The paltriness of the weekly rations, a sample of which is seen at the museum, is evi-dence of the plan to diminish the Jewish population deliberately. The weekly rations for each individual were minuscule, especially for one forced to perform hard labor. Women were not excluded from the toil; Edna Ipson was made to shovel coal into trains. She was not quick enough to suit a Nazi guard; therefore, he split open her head with the butt of his rifle. She wrapped a towel around her head and walked for miles to reach the hospital and have the hole sutured. She had no tempera-ture the next day, so her presence was demanded at the coal pile.

The painfully hungry resi-dents of the ghetto bore the effects of their own starvation and the hardship of watching their loved ones starve and deteriorate with sicknesses such as typhus and cholera.

Mec, pronounced "Mack," a teenaged friend of the Ipsons, tried to smuggle one loaf of bread to his severely ill, starv-ing mother. When he was caught, the punishment he received was death by hanging. Everyone in the ghetto was col-lected to view the sight.

A sewing machine was a valuable commodity on the outside to trade for food. Related photos on Page 32.

Everyone who visits the Virginia Holocaust Museum can see a replica of Mec hanging from the gallows.

The persecution of European Jews was not limited to their physical sustenance.

The Ipson family attended Nieh Shul (New Synagogue). One day, the Nazis issued a command for the residents to take their pets to the synagogue. Their obedience was rewarded with the slaughter of these animals inside the house of worship. The cruel vileness of this act was two-fold: Nazis killed the pets loved by Jewish families, and the blood from the deed rendered Nieh Shul unclean for worship. The fur from the pets was used for the gloves and earmuffs of the German military. The meat returned to the families in the form of rations.

Existing in the ghetto was one step from impossible. Starvation and disease claimed many lives. Periodic selections claimed many more.

Mec was hung with the noose under his chin, resulting in a slower death.

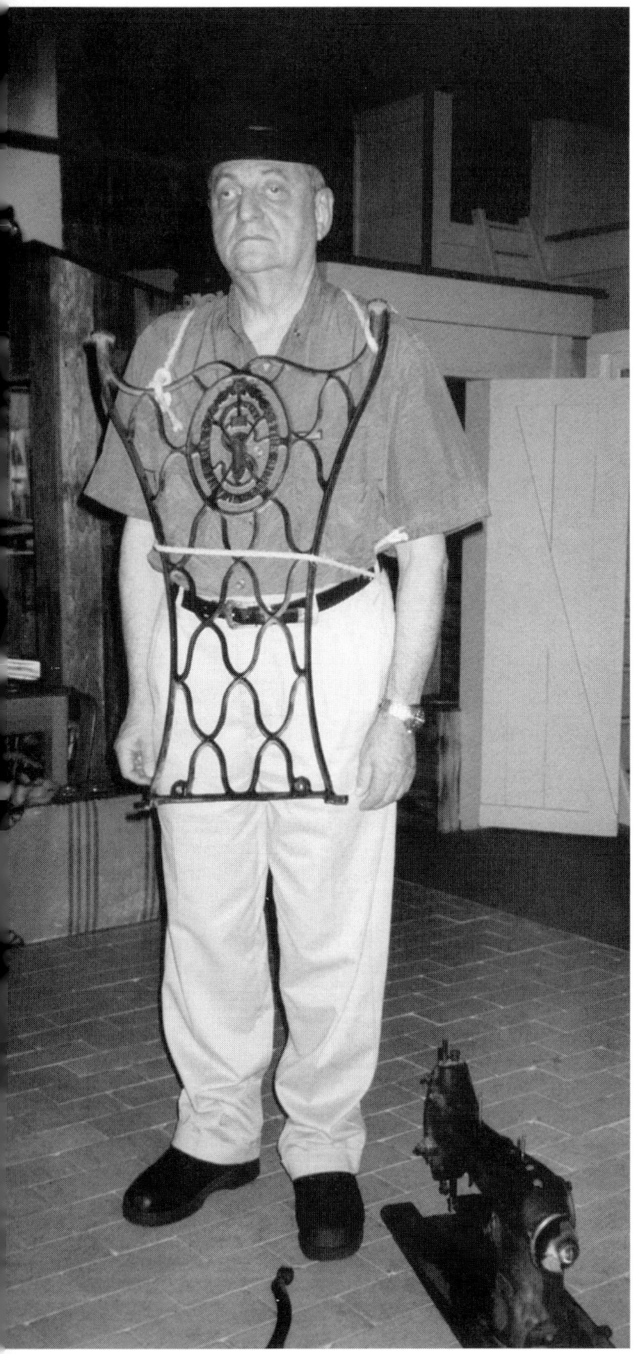

The sewing machine was disassembled with the flat sides and top of the stand strapped to the smuggler as a sandwich board. With these parts hidden under a coat, the worker/smuggler hoped to pass through the gate undetected.

The heavy machine itself was hung from the shoulders and suspended between the legs. Wearing a long coat, the smuggler took the machine past the guards.

CHAPTER EIGHT

USEFUL OR WORTHLESS: SELECTION IN DEMOCRATIC SQUARE

A s a resident of Kovno Ghetto, you enter Democratic Square and join a line that leads to SS Sergeant Helmut Rauca. The date is October 28, 1941, and you are one of 27,000 individuals commanded to wait your turn to state your profession. After hearing your answer, Sergeant Rauca will direct you with his riding crop to the left or the right. Your heart jumps within your chest at his voice—a voice that is your death knell, or the postponement of it.

The men dismissed to the left with their families were usually the professionals. The Nazis' opinion of the educated classes was that they provided nothing beneficial. The 9,200 formally educated Jews who had worked as doctors, lawyers, teachers, musicians, and the like would march to imprisonment in the Ninth Fort, which had been built during the nineteenth century and became a center for genocide during World War II. The very next morning, the prisoners were compelled to remove all clothing, stand naked at the edge of a mass grave, and await a bullet in the back of the head. Their clothing and personal effects, considered useful to German citizens, were taken from them. Their lives were taken as well because they were considered useless.

During another selection of the strong, 10,500 Jews whose bodies were not suited to Nazi labor requirements were murdered. The children who became orphans that day were hidden in the ghetto hospital in an attempt to save their lives. When guards discovered this, they locked the doctors, nurses, patients, and children inside the hospital, then set it ablaze.

At the outset of the Nazi occupation of the city, more than 500 young scholars had been tricked into gathering for their own execution. Thinking they would be contributing to

A low-ranking member of the dreaded SS made life-and-death decisions for Kovno inhabitants.

Israel Ipson replaced the universal joint of a Nazi vehicle, securing his family's safety for a while longer.

an archival project, they assembled and were marched to their deaths at the Ninth Fort. Dead men lead no revolutions.

Sergeant Rauca's line on October 28 will determine which Jews in Kovno Ghetto will temporarily evade execution. If he sends you to the right, you will be allowed to live another day. The sparing of a life is not done out of sympathy but out of the desire for labor. The men who were skilled in a trade would be kept around to work for their captors. They would remain in the ghetto for as long as their usefulness remained.

Jay Ipson's father, Israel, stood in that line and was required to tell Sergeant Rauca his profession. He was a lawyer, but he knew lawyers would be perceived as holding no worth for the Nazis. He claimed to be an automobile mechanic, and he kept his life.

Israel's answer would be tested the next day by a Nazi who showed up at his door to call for the mechanic. Israel kissed his family goodbye before leaving, for he knew the penalty for failure could be execution.

Lying underneath a Nazi's truck at the airport, he found a problem with the drive shaft of the automobile. Israel was inexperienced in automobile mechanics and wanted to ask advice from someone familiar with the trade. He said he would complete the task in a few days, but the Nazi wanted the repairs made at once. Israel was able to remove the universal joint and replace it with a part from the airport shop, using tools the clerk gave him. The Nazi who demanded the work of Israel Ipson made him shop foreman and promised a reward of bread and butter. Israel had not forgotten how Mec had been hanged for taking home food. He turned down the offer but was given the food just the same.

Despite Israel Ipson's accomplishment, safety in the ghetto was precarious. The Nazis' perception of a man's usefulness decided the length of time he would live. The paltry rations produced a slow death, and there was no preparation possible for the brutal punishments, such as the one inflicted on Edna Ipson.

Death in Kovno Ghetto was almost certain. The greatest chance for survival lay beyond its barbed wire.

Through an opening cut in the ghetto fence, Jay was the first to slip out across the street in the pitch-black night.

CHAPTER NINE

INESTIMABLE PRICE OF LIFE: REFUGE AT PASKOVSKIS' FARM

Sacrifice can be described as the relinquishing of something held dear. Sometimes, however, sacrifice is simply the willingness to do so.

In 1943, Jay Ipson was nearly nine years old, and his family had been residing in the ghetto since 1941. Edna Ipson's uncle, Itzak Kalamitsky, had been a farmer in Lithuania, and on childhood visits to his home she had become acquainted with a farmer named Martzuk, pronounced "Maar-chook." When Israel Ipson was assigned mechanical duties at the airport, he began to see Martzuk, who came to town to sell produce. Martzuk knew that attempting to help or sheltering an escapee promised execution if he were caught. Nevertheless, he told Israel that he would hide Jay if the boy could be removed from the ghetto.

Around the time of Martzuk's offer, Kovno Ghetto was turned into a concentration camp, and thousands of Jews were deported. Jay and several members of his family—his mother, her parents, and her three siblings—were to be sent to Riga Ghetto in Latvia. A Jewish police officer who was a friend of theirs took Jay and Mrs. Ipson from the deportees' line before they climbed into the truck. The rest of Mrs. Ipson's family did board the truck, and each one was killed in the Holocaust.

When night had fallen on November 26, 1943, the family met near the bridge that crossed Paneriu Street and linked two sections of the ghetto. They waited until the guard on patrol was farthest from them before Israel Ipson's cousin, Israel Gillman, cut out their exit in the barbed wire. The family crawled through and left the ghetto behind.

Martzuk met them and transported them by wagon to his home for a few days before the family departed for a farm set deeper in the countryside. Paskovskis' Farm was located in Trakau, eighty-five km (fifty-three miles) from Kovno, and was owned by a Polish-Catholic family. Mr. and Mrs. Paskovskis and their son, Stanislovas Krivicius, lived in a one-

Inmates needed to time their escape to avoid detection by guards on duty.

room home and slept in a single bed kept by the fireplace for warmth.

The Paskovskis tended crops such as potatoes and wheat, used to make bread; and livestock—pigs, chickens, and sheep. The sheep's wool contributed to the family's hand-made clothing. When the animals had been sheared during the winter, the Paskovskis let them inside to keep them out of the cold.

It was in this home of kindness that the Ipsons found refuge. For three weeks, they lived in the house while Israel Ipson dug a hiding place between two storage holes for potatoes. Once while he was working, the roof collapsed. Stanislovas' German shepherd, Rexxy, realized that Israel needed help. As Stanislovas was returning at 1 a.m. from playing the fiddle at a hoedown, Rexxy's barking signaled to the teenager that something was wrong, and Stanislovas was able to save Israel from being buried alive. That rescue was not the last time the dog would sound a notice of danger. Whenever strangers approached the potato hole, Rexxy barked to alert the Ipsons.

Rexxy will bark at you, too, as you head toward the potato hole from the museum's re-creation of the farmhouse. It was at a place like this—simple, one room, dirt-floored—that one family sacrificed their right to protect their own lives because another family had the right to be protected.

The three Ipsons found sanctuary with three Catholics who valued human life.

A farm dog provided companionship and protection for a family in hiding.

Case holds items such as gold coins covered with wool and used as buttons on Mrs. Ipson's sweater.

CHAPTER TEN

WHATEVER IT TAKES TO SURVIVE: THE IPSONS' HIDING PLACE

You're crawling through a tunnel in darkness and feeling your way to whatever is next. Your heart's pace is quick, for you cannot be sure what you will find.

When you have light to see, the picture before you is bleak. Thirteen human beings inhabit an underground space twelve feet long, nine feet wide, and four feet high. Other family members had joined the Ipsons in the potato hole after receiving messages from them via Martzuk.

We can see the dimensions of home for five women, four men, and four children, but there was no light in the potato hole. The only oxygen, not even enough to keep a match burning, came from a pipe that opened into Rexxy's kennel. Young Jay had only one ball to amuse himself—a clean pig's bladder containing beans—and that toy did not last long. For six months, the Ipson family's neighbors were lice and fieldmice. They could not bathe or change clothes or use a proper toilet. Covered by the darkness of night, Israel Ipson and Itzak Kalamitsky risked capture in order to procure food for their families. Mrs. Paskovskis, though poor herself, baked bread for the families sheltered beneath her potato field.

The Ipsons' hiding place was a space far below the classification of "small": nobody, not even the children, could stand up straight in the potato hole. But the tiny place represented something far larger. Their hiding place contained the hope that its inhabitants would outlive Nazi power and that when they left it, the potato hole would never again be needed for anything but storing food.

Jay Ipson's grandchildren try to experience his underground life in the small hollowed-out hiding place.

Jay and his relatives endured daily boredom, tension, and fear for six months in an earthen burrow.

The rattling of young Jay's pig bladder toy was not well-suited for a confined area.

To leave the potato hole prematurely was to enter into the possibility of capture and death. Israel Ipson's cousin, Leibel Gillman, and his mother, Nesse, had been living in the hiding place but decided to return to the ghetto to help others escape. They were caught and made to strip themselves and dig their graves before dying.

Those who remained in the potato hole had no guarantee of safety. A German tank came to the area searching for a missing lawyer and came within half a mile of the hiding place. The Germans left, however, still looking.

Jay Ipson and his family would leave the potato hole in August 1944. Israel Ipson had on occasional nights gone to a neighboring farmer's house to listen to a news program on the radio. He learned of the Russians' location in proximity to the hiding place and was aware he should be listening for them. The family, underground, heard the tanks and vehicles, came out of the potato hole, and saw the Russians on the highway.

Before World War II began, about 228,000 Jews lived in Lithuania. When the country was liberated by Soviets, approximately 2,500 remained.

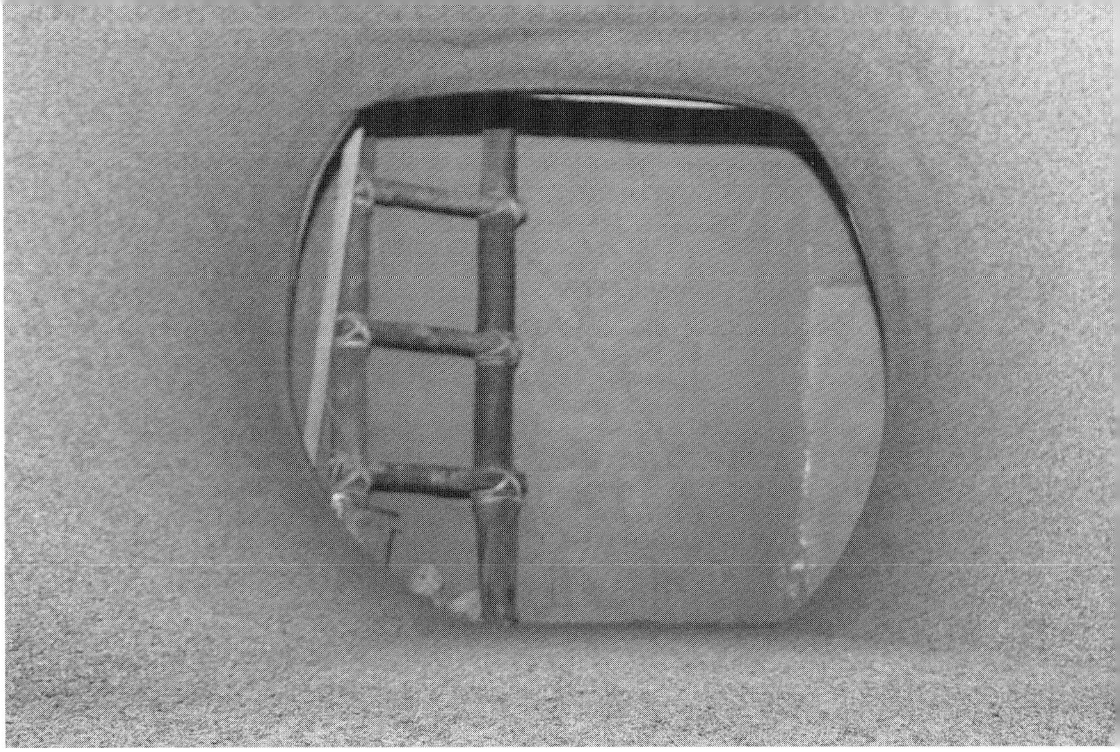

Crawling on hands and knees through a connecting tunnel, one could exit from the potato holes at either end.

Opening a false wooden bottom and raising the ladder allowed people to climb out.

CHAPTER ELEVEN

SOMETHING GREATER THAN PITY: THE HALL OF THE RIGHTEOUS

Martzuk and the other farmers who risked execution to save a family of Jews were among the many Gentiles who disagreed strongly enough with Hitler's murderous policies to do something more than shake their heads in sympathy.

In the Hall of the Righteous, the Virginia Holocaust Museum pays tribute to these men and women. They are the Righteous Among the Nations or the Righteous Gentiles. The term comes from a phrase in the Talmud, a Jewish text, that suggests that for whoever saves one life, it is as though he saved the world.

The individuals pictured in the Hall of the Righteous are not Jews, and many would have been free from Nazi persecution. By opening their lives and homes to their endangered neighbors, they risked retaliation by Nazis. They counted the cost, however, and decided that a human life, even one officially called worthless, is worth protecting.

They came from many countries. They were Catholics and Protestants, men and women, doctors and lawyers, priests and professors, businessmen, and homemakers.

Some Gentiles, such as the Paskovskis, hid whole families on their property—underground, under floors, in the attic, or behind false walls. Often a Jewish child would enter a Christian family to be raised as their own and included in religious acts and traditions. Although many Jewish chil-

Although the numbers of rescuers were small, our wall could never be long enough to honor those who did the right thing under adversity.

Stanislovas Krivicius (left) is honored at Yad Vashem in Israel for hiding thirteen Jews on his farm. The relatives of the Ipson family lived underground in a potato hole dug by Israel Ipson.

dren kept their lives in this manner, a large number were orphaned when their true parents were sent from the ghetto to die in the camps.

Another way of saving lives was through aid in emigration. While some figures in government were directing the massacre, others were trying to protect the intended victims. Some foreign diplomats, moved by the circumstances of the European Jews in the grip of Nazi power, arranged false passports and identification so Jews could find safety in other nations.

Swedish diplomat Raoul Wallenberg was responsible for saving tens of thousands of lives. Other non-Jews could save only one human being   or lost their lives trying.

But it is as if they saved the world.

CHAPTER TWELVE

UNDERGROUND WARRIORS: THE PARTISANS

When the German tank rolled frighteningly close to the Ipsons' hiding place, the soldiers were searching for the man they thought had escaped from Kovno Ghetto to lead a band of resistance fighters called partisans. These men and women lived in the forests of countries that the Nazis had invaded. They moved frequently and often had to say goodbye to family and friends. Though some entire families participated, others were separated when one member joined the guerrilla groups. Food was scarce, and danger was plentiful. A resistance fighter was always at risk of capture. The locals surrounding the forest might reveal the partisans' whereabouts for fear of punishment by Germans or because of their own anti-Semitism. It was highly probable that the partisans would die quickly if caught but would slowly die if interned in the ghettos and concentration camps.

The partisans launched surprise raids on their foes, exploded train tracks, attacked German convoys, and killed thousands of German soldiers. Other forms of warfare included the forging of documents, the distribution of anti-Nazi literature, and the aiding of Jewish escapees. Both Jews and non-Jews formed the guerrilla units, and some nearby villagers, though not fighting themselves, helped the partisans with food and assistance.

The Virginia Holocaust Museum displays the pictures of several men and women who took part in a very dangerous but invaluable cause. The partisans' relentless

Resistance depended on personal determination and often the availability of safety in forests, which Nazis were reluctant to enter.

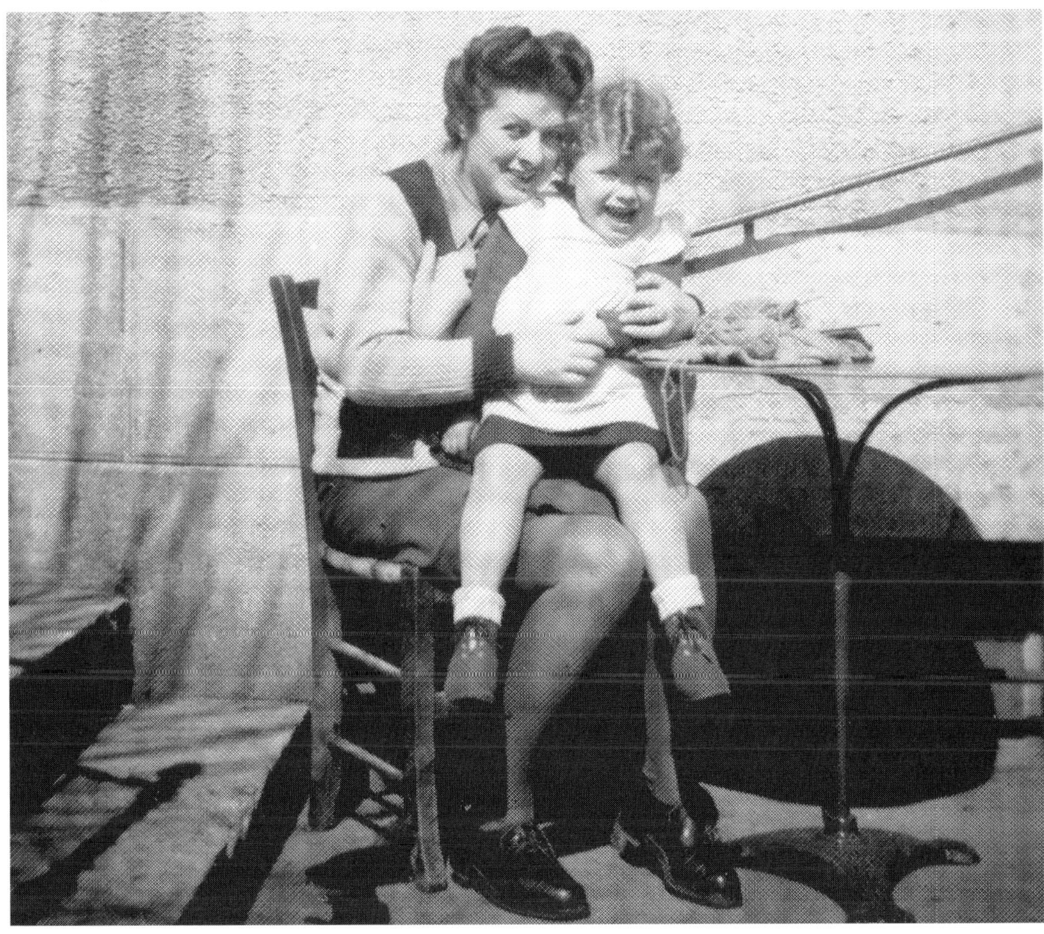

Ruth Marcus became a resistance fighter with the French Underground. In 1941 she placed her infant daughter, Yvonne, in a convent. After the war, Ruth was reunited with Yvonne.

efforts significantly hindered the German military and aided the Allied troops. Their contributions are inseparably linked with the outcome of the war.

The museum cannot show the face of every man and woman who participated in partisan warfare, but the pictures you see represent more than 30,000 individuals. Many were executed as traitors and foes. At the museum, though, they are together in the forests of Europe, brave and ready to fight. They prevail.

CHAPTER THIRTEEN

Death of the Innocents: The Children's Remembrance

C hildren are sometimes referred to as "innocents," an observation that the nature of a child is one of naïveté and artlessness. Children are most often powerless to design their own circumstances and ensure their own safety and can only rely on the kindness and protection of adults.

In the 1940s, while Aryan youngsters were being trained in Nazi dogma as part of Hitler Youth, 1.5 million non-Aryan children were being killed in Nazi-occupied countries. Their crime was being born into a family whose religion or politics did not match the Nazi ideal. They were enemies of the Reich.

No age was safe from slaughter. Unborn babies were killed when the expectant mother was shot to death. Young mothers cradled their infants before bullets entered both. The youngest children and those incapable of hard labor were killed, while older children awaited death in the ghettos and camps.

Other Jewish children were not sentenced to physical death, but they experienced the loss of all they had previously known and all the connections of their blood. Some who could pass as Aryan children were sent to German homes where they suffered the obliteration of ties to family, religion, and culture.

The Virginia Holocaust Museum presents actual drawings and poems produced by children who endured persecution that seems even colder when directed at the young. Children who had once been schoolmates of the children of guards and soldiers were now subject to death at the hands of those parents.

While not fully comprehending the reasons for their torment and fear, children were slaughtered—in far greater numbers than can be visualized.

The weight of the Holocaust's legacy is even heavier with the lives unlived. As many as 1.5 million children were not allowed to grow up, and millions more were forced to grow up at an accelerated rate because of incomprehensibly cruel experiences. Jewish children were told they were not good enough to play with non-Jewish peers. They witnessed executions. They were taken from their parents, and some never saw them again.

The children living in the Czechoslovakian ghetto Theresienstadt (Terezin) used their pencils to sketch armed guards, gallows, and deportations. Poignant poetry expresses ghetto life persistently hardening the heart of a child. Still, their art shows hope for something more: storks carry infants who will begin new lives, butterflies linger over flowers, and a rainbow arcs through the sky. There is a dream to meet people who will be nice, kind, decent.

Surviving children, though rushed into a brutal form of maturity, would live to encounter some bit of beauty and goodness again. Others would die, still chained to the horrors of the Holocaust, free in imagination only.

Images of murdered children scroll on a screen before the entrance to the cattle car.

Reflecting back against the brick wall, the children cry out to be remembered.

CHAPTER FOURTEEN

How to Answer the Jewish Question: The Final Solution

The "final solution." That formal phrase can be defined with the names of three million Jewish children, adults, and elders who perished in death camps, out of the more than six million who died in the Holocaust. The words "final solution" can be interpreted as the lives of three million people who entered gas chambers, which were disguised as showers, and were carried out to crematoriums.

Over lunch at the Wannsee Conference in January 1942, Nazi leaders discussed and clarified the blueprint for the Final Solution to the Jewish Problem. Earlier, from 1939 to 1941, they had perfected the extermination process used in death camps. They had gassed to death tens of thousands of mentally and physically handicapped children and adults in a "euthanasia" program—which closed, or was said to be, after public protest. During the Holocaust, the Nazis employed the gassing method to annihilate the group Hitler viewed as an even more serious threat to Aryan society: the Jews. Many of the early murders of Jewish Europeans had been committed by the Einsatzgruppen, mobile killing squads. These men would instruct the Jews of a region to gather on a particular day. Then, those assembled in a forest would dig a mass grave, and the squads would shoot each victim—man, woman, and child—at point-blank range. The

Train tracks led to death for Jews and other victims of Nazi philosophy and policy.

killing squad layered the bodies, some dead and many only wounded, in the mass grave. The sounds of labored breathing and the moans of the dying could be heard despite the stack of bodies above and around them.

The Einsatzkommandos often became depressed, suicidal, and insane from the absorption of so much death and blood in so intimate a way. For the good of these men, the Nazis devised a more detached way of killing.

The Virginia Holocaust Museum takes visitors through every forced step of the Final Solution. One can neither deny nor dull the panic that must have pulsated through the bodies of the victims. Though the guards endeavored to fool their prey, some Jews discerned that they would not exit the showers alive. There is not much resistance possible, however, when the guards are armed and you are not, and they push and propel and whip you, and dogs hound you toward your death in a stream of those who will die with you.

The manufacturers of Hess Königsberg ovens were so proud of their Nazi affiliation that they imprinted the SS lightning bolt symbol in place of any "s" in their name.

CHAPTER FIFTEEN

FROM ONE PRISON TO ANOTHER: THE BOXCAR

Emigration and expulsion were the early components of the plan to rid Germany of the Jews. But such measures were not possible once World War II began and Western European nations fell to German forces. Their populations, including the Jewish members, were now swept into the realm of Nazi authority.

The Reichsbahn, Germany's railway, had already borne those deported from their homes and corralled in ghettos or concentration camps. When the Final Solution was implemented, the boxcars would again be weighed down with a people hunted and enslaved. Millions of Jews boarded the trains. Many died before disembarking, and most others would survive only to face their end in the death camps.

Auschwitz-Birkenau, Sobibor, Treblinka, Belzec, Chelmno, and Majdanek were all located in Poland, a country in the center of Europe that had a convenient rail system and many anti-Semitic citizens. The camps would receive living, breathing Jewish families and would return burned bodies and careless mass graves.

Roundups in the ghettos forced one hundred people into boxcars the size of the reproduction inside the Virginia Holocaust Museum. The doors did not open from the inside, so the passengers were trapped, not knowing where they were going or when they would arrive. The darkness gave no clues to the destination. The journey could last half a day or half a week.

Upon exiting the cattle car and told to undress for a cleansing shower, men, women, and children suffered the final humiliation of disrobing together. •

Stuffed inside the narrow train with no space to move and a scanty supply of air to breathe, the inmates were finally released at one of the death camps. They left a rancid cattle car full of starved ghetto residents, many of whom had died but had nowhere to fall. They found guards who beat or sicced dogs on the weakened men, women, and children who did not exit with satisfactory speed. They were divided into the "not too weak to work" and the "ones not of service." The second group included the old, the ill, the young, the feeble, and the mothers or guardians of little children.

The first group would live a while longer. They would shower, be shaved, and change into a camp uniform. The second group would enter the next phase of the Final Solution.

Packed in a soiled and oppressive train car, prisoners were roughly prodded off and into lines that determined their fate.

CHAPTER SIXTEEN

THE FINAL SOLUTION FULFILLED: THE GAS CHAMBER

The Jews who exit the trains and fail the first selection are informed they will be deloused in a shower. They enter dressing rooms and are told to remove every piece of clothing and their shoes and to leave them there for retrieval afterwards. Members of both genders stand naked and wait; they are separated neither in the dressing room nor in the gas chamber.

The guards perpetuated the trickery about the purpose of the chambers by posting signs that directed Jews to the showers. They tried to keep the atmosphere calm in order to avoid arousing suspicion and instigating a revolt.

Once the Jews were securely locked inside the gas chamber, pellets of Zyklon B, a disinfectant, insecticide, and rat poison, were passed through vents in the roof or the wall. Because of the number of human beings crammed inside the chamber, the room's temperature rose, melting the pellets and releasing cyanide-based gas. With increased efficiency as a constant goal, the guards would eventually put in heating systems to help the pellets melt more quickly.

In other gas chambers, the guards used another poison, carbon monoxide, which they piped through the chamber wall from outside engines.

The process of moving inmates from the train to the gas chamber was intended to be calm and without hassles. Once the victims were locked inside, all ruses were unnecessary, calmness was impossible, and the room teemed with the hysteria of suffocating human beings. The dying clawed in vain at the

Through the window, guards could view the killing process, and the Sonderkommandos would know when death was complete.

Originally developed as a pesticide, Zyklon B pellets were poured into gas chambers through vents on the roof or side of building.

walls of their sealed tomb in an attempt to free themselves. Their marks remain in some chambers, a witness to generations today of the calculated murder of millions.

The museum's depiction of a gas chamber is small and stark and a place where our very nerves implore us not to linger. No pictures are necessary here; no words are adequate. To stand and to imagine the sudden awareness that you will never leave the room alive is to know the agony suffered by so many human beings in the last minutes of their lives. Their screams, pleas for mercy, weeping, fear, and despair had no power to save them. The echoes of those cries, however, have the power to change us if we will let ourselves listen when our bodies say, "Now I know how it felt."

CHAPTER SEVENTEEN

DESTROYING THE EVIDENCE: THE CREMATORY

The work of the poison was complete in less than half an hour. After the corpses, horridly twisted and discolored in death, were removed, the chamber was hosed down to be ready for the next group.

While Jewish families were being poisoned en masse, groups of Jewish men were charged with the disposal of the bodies. The work detail, called Sonderkommando, was responsible for shaving the corpses, locating any money, gold, jewels, or other valuables hidden on the bodies, taking the deceased by cart to crematoriums, and loading them inside the ovens. At times, one of the family members of a Sonderkommando was recognized among the dead, but mourning would not be tolerated. The men who completed this ghastly work had a life expectancy of only a few months, and they knew it. They must be killed to prevent their revealing the true purpose of the showers.

The items found by the work detail or left in the dressing room during the disrobing were stored in warehouses. The hair would be bundled and sold to private businesses for the making of socks for submariners and other products. The gold teeth were extracted from jaws broken for the removal. After being melted down, the gold was transferred to the Reichsbank. Items representing those stolen from the dead can be seen at the Virginia Holocaust Museum. The Nazis' victims were deemed more valuable in death than in life.

Sonderkommandos hosed out the gas chamber and pushed the bodies of their people into ovens.

Once the bodies had been stripped of all possible benefit, they were placed in the ovens. The mass graves used previously by the Nazis could not accommodate such large numbers of prisoners, and the ovens built by Topf und Sohne (Topf and Son) provided a way to hide the mass murder that was regularly taking place. The ash could be more conveniently discarded than entire bodies. The ovens were large enough to hold two or three corpses at once as time passed and starvation pared away the prisoners. The four to six pounds of a human figure left at the end of cremation were tossed into bodies of water, onto the forest floor, or into fields as fertilizer.

Half the Jews who died during the Holocaust were killed in the six extermination camps. Today, smoke from the crematoriums no longer fills the air of those camps, and visitors can take tours of some of the factories of genocide. The buildings are relics of a regime that decided the worth of human lives, and the bricks and mortar frame the evidence of memory for all whose value was considered dubious.

Case items represent personal effects taken from prisoners, extracted gold from teeth, hair, and a canister of Zyklon B pellets.

Hess Königsberg, one of eleven civilian companies, had the contract to manufacture crematorium ovens.

Ovens were specifically engineered to cremate mass numbers of human beings killed in camps.

CHAPTER EIGHTEEN

FIGURING OUT FREEDOM: LIBERATION

For one who has come through every stage of the Final Solution depicted in the Virginia Holocaust Museum, the body's relief at exiting that group of re-creations is almost palpable. It is an emotion not possible for the souls who were locked inside actual chambers, those who dug into the walls that imprisoned them and coughed up the gas that would kill them. The three million individuals who were murdered in the death camps went to their graves not knowing when the men who worked, starved, froze, and gassed them to death would see their power taken from them.

On July 23, 1944, the Russians liberated Majdanek. They would also free camps in the east, and American and British troops would liberate camps in the west in the spring of 1945. The Allied forces were met with the same grim portrait of malice in practice at each camp they entered. Frequently, records and documents had been burned and the guards had fled, leaving their captives alone in the desolate camps. The human beings the Allies encountered proved more than documents ever could the extent of the Nazis' disregard for so many human lives.

Thousands of corpses were piled near buildings, inside which survivors—skeletons that still held breath—showed with unmistakable clarity the forced starvation of the Nazi-imposed diet. Some survivors had been starved for so long that their bodies could not accept food when it was provided, and they joined the host of Jews massacred during the Holocaust. Other residents of newly liberated camps

American, British, Canadian and Russian troops liberated camps from July 1944 through May 1945.

were too sick to be healed even by the efforts of Allied troops and medical professionals.

The arrival of the liberators brought freedom to people who had been prisoners for years, but it was impossible to adjust immediately to the reality of that word. Freedom had been only a term, an idea, an imagined existence for so long, and now the prisoners were to accept it in its fullness.

Most soldiers were unprepared for the horrors they saw when they approached the gates.

For years, the camp survivors had witnessed organized murder, endured excruciatingly hard labor and compulsory starvation, and been treated as identity-less subhumans. For years, the survivors had watched family members and friends die. For years, the survivors had walked no farther than they were ordered to go and lived under the threat of execution if, without permission, they took a step outside the walls and barbed wire that enclosed them. For years, they had existed in a fortress meant not to protect its inhabitants but to prevent the extermination of them from being discovered and discontinued. What is freedom to someone who has not stopped to wipe the sweat from her brow because she might be beaten unconscious for her laziness and insubordination? What is liberation to someone who has watched a fellow prisoner fall to the frozen ground after hours of standing motionless as punishment for the blood he was born with? What is freedom to a woman whose entire family cannot celebrate this day with her? When captivity worse than any nightmare is fact, is freedom just an illusion?

Learning those answers would not come right away, but many internees were overwhelmed with the possibility to try. When Allied tanks began rolling in, the ever somber, putrid air of the camps was filled with weeping and laughter, as men and women were again permitted to embrace one another and their own emotions. Survivors scoured the guards' storerooms for food and possessions and gladly welcomed the care packages the troops distributed. Some soldiers, profoundly affected by the condition of the prisoners, gave of their own rations.

The Nazis, however, had seen to it that many prisoners would not live to see the day of liberation. As the Allies entered Poland and forced the German army back, the Nazis assembled camp residents for evacuation. The Jews were shot en masse or moved to camps farther from the approaching Allies. The Nazis wanted no living testimony to the depth of their depravity.

Though the ground was snow-covered, many Jews walked barefoot or with rags wrapped around their feet. Any who stumbled, fell, or walked too slowly were shot by the guards. The trips could cover hundreds of miles, and the Jews' unhealthy bodies often could not take the exertion. These death marches would claim the lives of many men and women just days before they would have been freed.

The Nazis forced prisoners to labor in camp workshops for the German war effort.

Although the marches were intended to forestall the discovery of the particulars of Nazi policy and often took place at night, the marches were not wholly absent from the public's gaze. Villagers saw the rag-clad human beings flanked and followed by armed guards, but they rarely offered assistance. At the war's close, both villagers living a few miles from the camps and citizens of countries in other parts of the world would try to excuse their inaction with a defense of ignorance and disbelief of the atrocities. When the Soviets entered Majdanek and walked on ground that had become a center of human extermination, they asked International Red Cross workers to photograph and describe the destruction. The pictures and the words were published, and disbelief continued. The documentation was considered Russian propaganda. When American and British forces reported the same accounts of the camps they entered, the global population finally began to reckon with the reality they had dismissed as horrific fiction.

General Dwight D. Eisenhower collected all the villagers he could from their homes near the camps so that they could see with their own eyes the degeneracy that had ruled for years just outside their homes. The neighbors of camp residents would be the ones to transport and bury bodies. Disbelief and ignorance would by necessity be buried also in that way.

Visitors to the Virginia Holocaust Museum have, in a way, toured the camps. As we walk past the barbed wire in the liberation area, we see the faces that met Allied troops. We see the weakness of men just trying to stand up at the approach of the liberators. We see the joy against the desolation, the celebration of release from the unthinkable, but the hesitancy of release into a now unfamiliar world.

We see the remembrances of servicemen who fought and freed the men and women that another group had striven to exterminate. We see the uniforms they wore and the medals that graced them.

Some men did not live to see their camps liberated, and some men did not live to see their comrades liberate the camps. The Jews who died remind us of the atrocities committed by one group of human beings against another in the name of their own superiority. The Allies who died remind us of the courage of human beings to stand in jeopardy for one another, even for those whom they do not know.

Despite the efforts of medical teams, some prisoners were so physically compromised that they could not survive.

American soldiers witnessed misery when they liberated Dachau and treated American POWs from Berga camp.

CHAPTER NINETEEN

In the Shadow of the Past: The Displaced Persons Camp

Germany had been defeated, and Hitler had committed suicide. The Nazi party no longer controlled the Jewish population of Europe, but the effects of that regime would linger even after its demise.

The living victims of the war's devastation received aid from the United Nations Relief and Rehabilitation Administration (UNRRA), which was established in November 1943 and for which Israel Ipson worked while in Munich, Germany.

Before leaving for the U.S., Jay Ipson, mother, Edna, and friends are photographed by his father, Israel, at Bremenhoffen.

Jews who had sought safety in hiding places or who had been imprisoned in camps often had no home to which to return. Their houses had been pillaged or inhabited* by strangers. Other survivors did not want to return to their old homes, for they had no family members to live there with them. Many who were able to return home returned to fierce anti-Semitism remaining in European communities. Forty-one survivors of the Holocaust were killed and fifty wounded during an anti-Jewish riot in Poland after the war.

Survivors who could not, for whatever reason, return home were called Displaced Persons (DPs) and lodged in former concentration camps, which could house large groups. Allied forces oversaw the camps, and the situation was to be temporary, until the Jews could gain entrance to other countries. But Jews were still not welcome or permitted past some borders. Full freedom had by no means

arrived. The conditions in the DP camps were often deplorable, and the former prisoners' memories of the brutality they had endured remained fresh due to their continued presence in the camps.

President Harry Truman sent lawyer Earl G. Harrison to examine the DP camps. The report he returned to Washington suggested that the only difference between the camps before and after the war was the elimination of the policy of extermination. His report led to greater attentiveness to Jewish Displaced Persons and the establishment of Jewish-only camps after instances of anti-Semitic violence in nonsegregated camps.

The shift toward segregated camps engendered other changes. New families began, as marriages took place in high numbers and the camps produced the highest birth rate of any location in Europe. Rabbis attended to the DPs' religious welfare. Teachers provided educational opportunities for school-age survivors, and adults acquired knowledge in such areas as farming and tailoring, which would increase their chances of securing income. Displaced Persons' camp newspapers were produced, and plays were performed. Rabbi Abraham J. Klausner gave the survivors the name Sh'erit ha-Pletah, "Surviving Remnant," a Biblical term. Families whose connections had been lost

Jay Ipson (front row, sixth from left) sits with children at a Munich rally supporting DP immigration into Palestine.

Alex Lebenstein of Richmond (second row, center) with kitchen crew at Degendorf DP camp in Bavaria.

A 1946 play performed at Degendorf gave survivors who waited to emigrate some enjoyment.

Lonia Wiatrak Itzkowitz, at age sixteen, worked as an interpreter handling complaints for the British Administration in the DP camp at Bergen Belsen.

found them again through tracing organizations and lists of names arranged by Rabbi Klausner and dispatched around the globe. The camps were not ideal, but the Jewish residents were doing their best in a very difficult situation until they could gain a true home of their own and a place of permanence in North or South America or British-controlled Palestine.

Because it might inflame the Arab inhabitants of the area, however, Britain refused Jewish immigration to Palestine. The DPs responded with protests and rallies to appeal to the world's population. They would press on until they received the attention and support they needed.

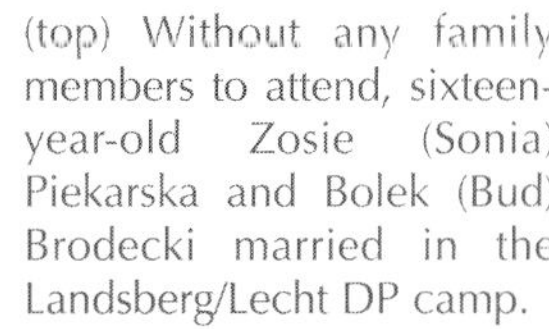

(bottom) Bud and Sonia Brodecki's son, Joseph, born December 12, 1946, in a DP camp, represented the renewal of Jewish life after the Holocaust.

(top) Without any family members to attend, sixteen-year-old Zosie (Sonia) Piekarska and Bolek (Bud) Brodecki married in the Landsberg/Lecht DP camp.

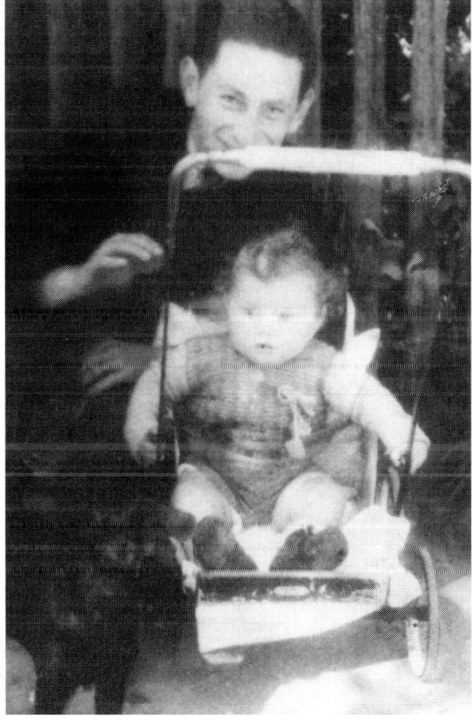

DP camp police badge worn by Bud Brodecki (top row), who served in the police force from July 1945 until September 1949.

CHAPTER TWENTY

HOPING FOR HOME:
HAGANAH SHIP EXODUS 1947

Prior to World War II, immigration policies affecting European Jews became strict and severe in nations besides Germany. Those restrictions placed on the Jewish population did not altogether disappear with the Nazi party. Finding somewhere to go—after the loss of homes, property, and loved ones—proved an onerous search in a world that still did not completely accept Jews. The establishment of a Jewish state in Palestine seemed to some the only way to have a lasting home, but that avenue was closed to the Jews as well and would be opened only with drastic measures.

Jack Bernstein and Israel November, two Jews living in Richmond, and friends of theirs in Richmond and Baltimore bought the *President Warfield*, a steamship from the Chesapeake Bay, and donated it to the Haganah, the precursor to the Israel Defense Force. The vessel left Sete, France, near Marseilles, in July 1947 and was renamed *Haganah Ship Exodus 1947* during a ceremony on board.

The objective was to transport 4,500 survivors to Palestine for illegal entrance onto the land, but the British Navy had been tracking the movements of the *Exodus* and stopped her close to Palestine.

Though unarmed, the Jews resisted the Navy, but the British crew's guns killed at least three passengers and wounded more than 150. The ship was rammed, and British marines came aboard. The crew of the *Exodus* surrendered, and the injured vessel was towed to Haifa. There the refugees were loaded onto prison ships and returned to

Exodus 1947 was one of about one hundred illegal ships attempting to bring survivors to Palestine.

President Warfield represents Virginia's role in helping Holocaust survivors create a homeland.

France on July 29, 1947, but they refused to leave the ships. On August 22, 1947, after almost a month at anchor, the prison ships were sent to the British Zone in Germany.

The men and women who had boarded the *Exodus* to mold a new life in Palestine were sent back to a life very much like the one they had survived. They were placed on trains that traveled to Poppendorf DP camp, in the very country that had organized and executed their captivity prior to and during World War II.

The insensitive, harsh treatment of the passengers of the *Exodus* tainted Britain's image in the eyes of much of the world and enlarged public support for the establishment of a Jewish state. The next year—in May 1948—the dream of a Jewish homeland would be realized.

Cases hold the sweater of a Jewish sailor and rucksack of a refugee from the *Exodus.*

Exodus 1947 VOYAGE

1- Baltimore, Maryland: November 4, 1946, Weston Trading Company, representing Haganah, pays $50,000 to rescue *Warfield* from scrap heap. Crew sails ship to Norfolk, where Moon Engineering Company refits ship.

2- Cape Hatteras, North Carolina: Crew sails *Warfield* under Honduran flag to Hatteras in a series of evasive maneuvers. British agents are aware of Haganah agenda.

3- Norfolk, Virginia: From port of departure on February 25, 1947, *Warfield* sets sail for Europe, encounters storm seventy-five miles out, and takes on water.

4- Philadelphia, Pennsylvania: U.S. Coast Guard escorts listing *Warfield* to Philadelphia for repairs. Four weeks later, *Warfield* sets out shadowed by British ships.

5- Ponta Delgada, Azores: British denies *Warfield* chance for refueling at Azores. Under cover of darkness, crew steals some fuel and sails out.

6- Marseille, France: *Warfield* sails to Marseille in evasive maneuver.

7- Port de Bouc, France: *Warfield* sails to Port de Bouc in evasive maneuver.

8- Portovenere, Italy: *Warfield* is refitted to accommodate about 4,554 passengers. British demand that Italians prevent departure.

9- Port de Bouc, France: *Warfield* sails to Port de Bouc in evasive maneuver.

10- Sete, France: *Warfield* arrives July 9. Haganah arranges for 4,554 Jews from DP camps in Germany and Poland to converge at port. Yielding to British demands to halt departure, French officials arrive as *Warfield* sets sail on July 11, shadowed by five British warships.

11- Haifa, Palestine: British attack *Exodus 1947* during night of July 18 in international waters. Crew surrenders after struggle, and *Exodus* is towed to Haifa. Immigrants are put on three British prison ships, *Runnymede Park, Ocean Vigour,* and *Empire Rival.*

12- Port de Bouc, France: France refuses to force immigrants off ships. Five die and only 130 sick disembark. After a few weeks British officials order ships back to Germany.

13- Hamburg, Germany: September 7, prison ships moor at British-occupied Hamburg dock after seventeen-day voyage. Only half disembark, and British officers forcibly remove remaining people. Holocaust survivors are returned to camps near Poppendorf, fifteen miles from Hamburg.

A mothballed ship turned into a symbol of deliverance as it sailed to various ports for repair, renovation, and rescue.

CHAPTER TWENTY-ONE

Homeless Still: Cyprus

The 4,500 passengers of the *Exodus* were not the only Jews to attempt to enter Palestine illegally. The majority of those caught were transported to Cyprus to be housed in detention camps that opened in August 1946. The Mediterranean island was under British control and was closer to Palestine than Europe was. During the camps' existence, a total of 51,000 refugees on Cyprus spent time in a situation that resembled too closely their experiences during the Holocaust.

Once again, they faced poor sanitation, along with infection and skin disease, caused by overcrowding and a water shortage. The Virginia Holocaust Museum shows the difference between the summer camps, consisting of tents, and the winter camps, a group of tin huts. Both sorts of housing were less than basic, and there were too many prisoners for Britain's finances. At that country's request, religious assistance, medical workers, and food arrived from the Joint Distribution Committee in America.

Quonset huts were winter shelters for Jews whose attempts to reach a homeland were frustrated.

The improvement in care helped somewhat but could not quench the inmates' desire for Palestine. Although the State of Israel would be established in May 1948, the camps on Cyprus would not close until February 1949. The detainees were subject to a United Nations embargo that thwarted them from helping Israel fight for security.

Holocaust refugees were again imprisoned in camps as guards watched from towers.

Summer tents offered lodging while Jews waited to be let into the new State of Israel.

CHAPTER TWENTY-TWO

THE LAND OF PROMISE: PALESTINE/ISRAEL

The forced emigration and deportation of Europe's Jewish population in the early twentieth century was not the first dispersion of the Jewish people. In A.D. 70, during Roman rule, Jews were forced from Israel and scattered across the Roman Empire. The homeland from which they had been exiled holds a strong attachment for many Jewish people. Since the establishment of the Jewish faith, Israel has possessed spiritual and cultural importance of extraordinary magnitude.

Though living in lands far from Israel, many Jews desired to return. The area was renamed Palaestina (Palestine) in A.D. 132, but its significance remained the same. Its attraction was powerful, and Jews began returning to Zion in considerable numbers from 1190 on. They were often persecuted in the countries to which they had been exiled, and they desired a place where they could feel at home and not be abused and unwanted.

From the shores of Palestine, British soldiers watch as an illegal survivor ship is forced into harbor.

The worst persecution of the Jewish people would occur under Adolf Hitler and the Nazi party during the Holocaust. The barbarity with which European Jews were treated at that time would drive the establishment of a Jewish state from desire to reality. Ironically, one man and his minions had sought to annihilate the Jewish race, but in part because of the world's disgust at their deeds, the State of Israel would be founded.

In the 1890s, a Jew named Theodor Herzl, who had witnessed acts of anti-Semitism in Europe, founded the World Zionist Organization and called for Jews to return to their homeland. The movement called Zionism sought to unify European Jews toward the goal of a Jewish nation in the land now known as Palestine. The Zionist movement was assisted by the global reaction to the Holocaust and the realization of the great need for a Jewish state. The campaign for its establishment gained supporters around the world and in the United Nations General Assembly.

Agreement with the idea, however, was not universal. The land was populated by large numbers of Arabs, many of whom wanted not a single Jew to reside in Palestine and who declared absolute hostility and opposition to the establishment of a Jewish state. Acting out of fear of repercussions between Jews and Arabs, the British government forbade large-scale immigration to Palestine. But continued anti-Semitism in Europe, the riots and murders of Jews, and the conditions of the DP camps strengthened the resolve of many Jews to enter the area.

Great Britain pulled out of Palestine in 1948, and on May 14 of that year, a Jewish state, Israel, was created. The Law of Return was enacted, which granted automatic citizenship to all returning Jews.

Well prior to the day Israel's prime minister, David Ben-Gurion, signed the nation's Declaration of Independence, Israel was fighting for sovereignty. Tension existed, exploding into violence, between Jews in Palestine and Arabs angry at their presence. On May 15, 1948, armies from Israel's Arab neighbors attacked the fledgling nation during the War of Independence, which would last until 1949.

Although Israel was victorious in that conflict, the strife between Israelis and Arabs would not end. Discord between the two groups continues today and is reported in newspapers and on television news programs. Both the Arabs in Palestine and the Israelis believe the land belongs to them, and they are willing to fight fearlessly for victory. The Jews of Israel have a history of being made to battle for a home and are accustomed to the demands of the struggle.

CHAPTER TWENTY-THREE

THE CRIMINALS' RECOMPENSE: THE HALL OF JUSTICE

The faces of the men responsible for the atrocities of the Holocaust are not the focus of the Virginia Holocaust Museum, but in the Hall of Justice we see those faces and read the names of several men whose actions have already been described. After the war, they were brought to court to be held accountable for their crimes. Judges from the Allied nations—Great Britain, France, the Soviet Union, and the United States—presided over the Nuremberg Trials, held in Nuremberg, Germany, in 1945.

Twenty-two war criminals were brought before the court, and the verdicts resulted in twelve death sentences, three life imprisonments, four prison sentences, and three acquittals. Subsequent Nuremberg proceedings took place in the latter 1940s, and other trials were held in countries besides Germany, including in Israel.

Adolf Hitler, the architect of the extermination of the Jewish people and other "undesirables," committed suicide toward the close of the war, along with Joseph Goebbels, the Nazi minister of propaganda, who instigated Kristallnacht. Heinrich Himmler, the director of the Final Solution, also killed himself.

Many other Nazis never stood trial, having fled Germany for America, Argentina, Canada, Great Britain, and other countries. As determined as they were to evade justice, however, so determined were other individuals to see justice served. SS bureaucrat Adolf Eichmann, Sergeant Helmut Rauca, and Auschwitz doctor Josef Mengele are among the Nazi criminals chased by a dedicated group who have spent the decades since the war finding the men who sought to escape the consequences of their crimes.

The defendants who did face the judges at Nuremberg could not claim they were innocent because they had simply followed orders. The tribunal emphasized that each human being is responsible and accountable for his own actions.

The guards of the camps, the members of the killing squads, and the top Nazi officials had been given a choice to succumb to evil or to stand up to it. In "following orders," they supported evil with all their being, and they were as guilty as the masterminds.

Chief of the Luftwaffe, Colonel General H. J. Stumph, surrenders with Field Marshal Wilhelm Keitel, commander in chief of the German Armed Forces (with sword). Keitel justified the massacres by Einsatzgruppen (Special Action Squads) in Russia and said, "Any act of mercy is a crime against the German people." He was executed in 1946. *Courtesy of National Archives still pictures, U.S. Army photo*

CHAPTER TWENTY-FOUR

Never Forget: The Survivors' Room and the Tower of Remembrance

There is one room at the museum where it is evident that visitors are intended to linger. It is not to be rushed through, overlooked, or ignored. It is the Survivors' Room, where photographs and letters are visible, readable proof of the experiences of men and women who now reside in Virginia. The space is akin to a living room, where guests sit and stay and listen to the stories of elders. In this case, the stories have been recorded and play on a television set so that visitors can hear survivors of the Holocaust choose their own words and describe in their own way what happened to them on the continent of Europe between 1933 and 1945.

Their stories bespeak the affront of Nazi propaganda and the manifold components of persecution, including prejudice, separation, and dehumanization. They speak of death camps and labor camps; of going into hiding and of fighting for the resistance; of freedom at last.

They survived what so many others did not.

The Holocaust divided families into the living and the dead and friendships into the mourning and the mourned.

Although the survivors have been granted the years to pass on their stories, the loss of life all around them changed their lives, and the deaths of those who were closest to them impoverished them.

A Star of David entrance leads into the tower that holds photos of murdered Virginia family members.

Though men and women now, many children who lived through and survived the Holocaust had to face the rest of their days without their parents or grandparents or brothers or sisters, who live now only in the memory of those who love them and whom they loved. The Virginia Holocaust Museum gives the dead a place of honor, lest the world forget those who paid the price of human suffering and life itself during one of the darkest times in history.

The Tower of Remembrance, designed by Al Rosenbaum, is their memorial. Virginia residents who lost relatives during the Holocaust donated the pictures. The tower contains a stained-glass window to depict the flames of the Holocaust and to represent Mount Sinai. The word "zachor" means "remember." Remember the men and women and children who cannot ask you to remember their lives. Remember that the little boys used to play leapfrog and the little girls used to twirl in their good dresses. Remember that the mothers used to encase their children in hugs, and the fathers tried to do for their families all that they could. Remember.

These two spaces, the Survivors' Room and the Tower of Remembrance, keep close to home the losses sustained and the lives forever altered. They connect the past to the present and the dirt of Europe to the Virginian soil on which we stand.

They connect those who survived with those who did not and those of us who experienced none of it with those who experienced the worst of it.

Light through the tower's stained glass window shines down on loved ones lost forever.

Plaques honor donors who pledge their support for the museum's mission.

Visitors take time to sit and listen to Virginia survivors tell their stories.

The tour concludes at the end of the tracks as visitors now become witnesses.

CHAPTER TWENTY-FIVE

BACK THEN, HERE NOW: THE CATTLE CAR

The trip through the Virginia Holocaust Museum begins at the train station, where Jewish men, women, and children boarded the trains that would deport them to ghettos and concentration camps. The trip concludes at the cattle car, which was acquired by the museum in 2003 from Haltern am See, Germany. The car was built in the early 1900s and existed in Holocaust-era Germany. Although it is not possible to know if this particular cattle car carried Jews to their deaths, it is known that it showed evidence of extensive travel.

The German cattle car is now parked on Richmond's East Cary Street, in front of the museum. Benches inside allow visitors to ponder all they have seen and learned. Votive candles may be carried to the museum or purchased in its shop, and the lighting of each candle signifies a promise never to forget.

The cattle car is no longer used to transport tightly packed human beings to concentration camps, and it is no longer a traveling coffin for the individuals who died during the journey. Its purpose now is for something diametrically opposed to the depravity and destruction it served in years past. Its purpose now is to be an instrument of education and remembrance and to honor the dead by inspiring the living.

Signs on the entrance gate alert visitors to the dread experienced by those about to encounter Nazism.

Those who now enter the cattle car know where they will be going when they leave it, and no armed guard will yank them down the steps. You are free to walk inside to sit and to think and—when a train rolls along on the tracks above the nearby canal and the sound reaches your ears—to imagine that you are one of the number being relocated to a future that would have been impossible to imagine.

A symbol of despair and destruction stands outside the museum as a reminder of what hate can do.

Candles inside the cattle car are lit as a memorial to six million. Hebrew letters above candles tell visitors to "remember."

The symbolic rumble of a train rolling by the entrance will stay with visitors long after it passes.

Witnesses leave the Virginia Holocaust Museum and take with them a new wisdom.

EPILOGUE

Six million lives. Six million human beings who were born into families, who gave and were given love and who meant something to someone. Not six million subhuman creatures whose presence plagued society, but six million individuals with a beat in their heart and air in their lungs. They lived and they died. They were mourned and were—and still are—missed. Each death added one more tally mark to the score of man's inhumanity to man, and each death subtracted from the world a life given the breath for something more than to be four to six pounds of ashes. It is impossible to know what those men, women, and children would have done and who they would have become. But whatever it was, they were, and they would have been.

With each life lost, the human race lost what it could never replace, and the ever-widening hole still snakes its way through the faces of humankind. Some do not know it exists, and some think it cannot come near enough to touch them. But it is a hole of abbreviated heartbeats and interrupted pulses, and because it contains what is essential for all of us, it has some part of each of us.

To ask why a person in the twenty-first century or a member of a group not singled out for slaughter should care about what happened during the Holocaust is to not recognize the extent of the suffering. It is to forget that other human beings—not machines—performed the murder of millions. Those who killed families had families of their own. It is to disbelieve that any ethnicity or class or group of people is immune from hatred. But what happened to one can happen to another.

The past cannot be changed. The stolen lives cannot be restored, and the barbarous cruelty cannot be undone. The Nazis cannot be prevented from carrying out the horrors of the Holocaust.

But each human being alive today has control over one life and over what is done with it. To give honor and the dignity of remembrance to those who suffered and perished is a feat able to be achieved. It is imperative to remember—so as not to repeat—the Holocaust.

Each human being can know and understand that a person is so much more than what we see, and his life is so much more than the brief moments we spend in it. We are never aware of all that anyone around us has survived or overcome or is overcoming. We owe, both to him and to ourselves, patience and compassion and consideration.

Many of the most brutal acts perpetrated by man against man during the Holocaust are not recorded in this book. Let them not be lived out in the world around you.

RESOURCES OF THE VIRGINIA HOLOCAUST MUSEUM

Most visitors to the Virginia Holocaust Museum never enter several other rooms located there, but they are an important part of the museum's mission to educate and inform the public.

A research library of approximately 4,000 books on the Holocaust is open during museum hours. The library, which does not lend out its texts and does not and will not contain any fiction, is available for anyone who wants to learn more about a grave period in history.

There is a studio where interviews with survivors, witnesses, and liberators are conducted and taped. The tapes are contained in the museum's video library, and the testimonies can be viewed on the premises.

The Holocaust Education Resource Center offers a wide range of print material and audio and video files for on-site research.

Teachers come to the museum's classroom to receive tips on presenting information about the Holocaust to their students. Community meetings are held in the classroom as well.

A larger meeting area is the auditorium, which is a reproduction of Lithuania's Choral Synagogue. The auditorium is also used for teaching sessions as well as weddings, bar mitzvahs, and other gatherings.

Trained personnel tape oral histories for future generations.

For more information about any of the museum's resources or facilities or to schedule group visits, call (804) 257-5400. For a teacher's guide, visit the museum's website at www.va-holocaust.com.

Professors from local universities and area Holocaust educators conduct annual training workshops for teachers.

(above) Reflecting on the Deuteronomy verse encourages educators and parents.

(below) Teaching aids, maps, and posters hang in the classroom.

Auditorium contains the reproduction of Choral Synagogue in Lithuania with balcony panels from a former Richmond synagogue.

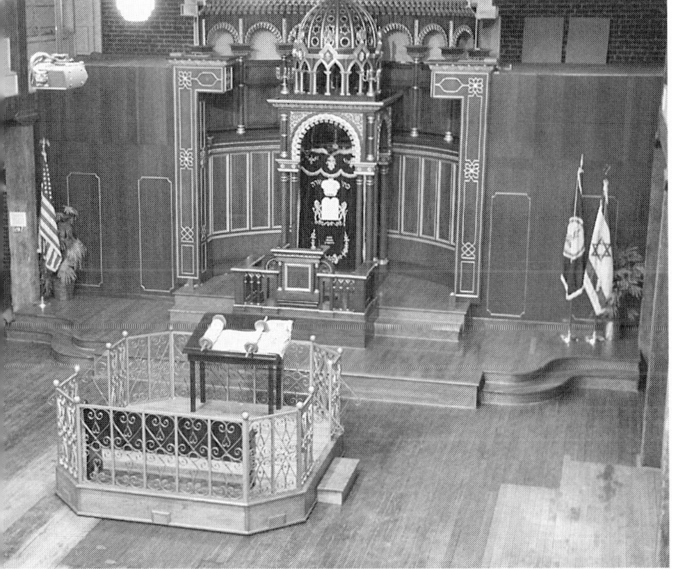

View of Choral Synagogue bima (altar area) and chuppa (canopy) shows Jay Ipson with Isaeli visitors reading a Torah scroll (the five books of Moses) that survived the Lithuanian Holocaust.

School classes and large groups meet for tour orientation and debriefing in the auditorium. The opera *Brundibar*, originally performed in Terezin camp, was presented in February 2005 for schools and the general public.

Visitors are greeted with an explanation of the museum. Docent tours and book and audio guides are available.

The museum shop is open daily, offering a selection of Judaica and creations from local artists.

A wide selection of Holocaust-related children's and adult books is available.

"THANK YOU FOR TELLING YOUR STORY"

–QUOTATIONS FROM THE VIRGINIA HOLOCAUST MUSEUM GUEST BOOK

The Virginia Holocaust Museum has welcomed visitors from cities across Virginia, from more than forty other states, and from several other countries including Australia, Canada, England, France, Germany, Israel, Mexico, and Sweden.

It is requested that each visitor sign the museum's guest book at the end of the tour. A sampling of quotations from recent visitors has been collected on these pages. Their words describe an experience still very fresh in their minds, hearts, and bodies. "Very moving," "very powerful," and "thank you" are often the only message that can be written.

"Brought tears to our eyes and chill bumps."
—A Raleigh, North Carolina, couple

"It is a very powerful experience to walk through these rooms and experience the exhibits. There is a part of me that cannot take it all in at the moment."
—A woman from Oregon

"Very interesting and moving! Well done. A great way to make us aware of what happened—so that we can stand up for others—so that it will not be repeated!!"
—A Greenville, Virginia, woman

"Very touching—everyone needs to see this exhibit!"
—A woman from Crozet, Virginia

"Wonderfully informative, sensitive, emotional."
—A woman from Charlottesville, Virginia

"Amazing! Very educational. Intense!"
—Visitors from West Virginia

"I was fascinated and enjoyed learning new things."
—*A young lady from Louisiana*

"Opens your eyes. Incredible!"
—*A young man from Florida*

"Thank you for this excellent portrayal of one of our worst times in history. We should not forget."
—*A woman from New York*

"Very moving and stirring—effectively designed and organized to stir the mind and soul."
—*A Great Falls, Virginia, man*

"I love this museum. The tour was excellent! We got a feeling of what Jews had to go through every day."
—*A teenager from Chester, Virginia*

"Well done. We must never forget!!! Let us be humane to our fellow man."
—*A man from New York*

"Powerful! Memorable! Intimate portrayal of this awful time in our history."
—*A New York couple*

"Opened my eyes to all the persecution that really went on."
—*A man from Ashland, Virginia*

"We had never heard about what happened afterwards."
—*A family from Georgia*

"We learned a lot more than we could have learned in the history books."
—*A youth ministry from North Carolina*

"Thank you for helping us know. We need to never forget!!!"
—*A woman from Raleigh, North Carolina*

"Gave me cold chills to think of what these people went through. Will be back."
>—*An Ashland, Virginia, woman*

"Overwhelming."
>—*A Missouri couple*

"Very emotional and very impressive. We will remember."
>—*A couple from Spring Grove, Virginia*

"It was extremely interesting to see and hear real survivors talk about their experiences. If you need some volunteers, call me."
>—*A Richmond teenager*

"Thank you for the time and effort that were put into this museum. The feelings felt here and the realization of the horror that happened are indescribable. But we do appreciate knowing and now being able to help this to never happen again."
>—*A Richmond family*

"I am glad I took my son here!"
>—*A Chesterfield, Virginia, visitor*

"A painful memory that is still very much alive within me."
>—*An older man from Yorktown, Virginia*

"It was very sad and realistic and sometimes scary, but it really happened!"
>—*A young person from Richmond*

"My great-grandparents are in the Tower of Remembrance."
>—*An Ashland, Virginia, girl*

"Although I had known a lot about the Holocaust, the presentation opened my eyes, and I have greater respect for those who died as well as those who survived."
>—*A Richmond woman*

"Amazing. Everyone should visit. Reading and watching movies cannot compare to physically experiencing exhibits, which so clearly communicate the horror."

—A Philadelphian

"Excellent work. Keep it up. People should know about this. The sufferings of these people shouldn't be forgotten. Like Bosnia and Herzegovina."

—A young woman from Herzegovina

"We will never forget this experience."

—Visitors from New York

"Cannot speak."

—A man from King William, Virginia

"The interactive aspect of the museum affected me emotionally."

—A man from El Paso, Texas

"Awesome and inspiring. One of the finest of the many Holocaust museums we've been to."

——A couple from Potomac, Maryland

"As an African American and Native American, I felt shaken to the core about man's inhumanity to man—however, I felt I could relate. I admire the commitment of Jewish people to continue to remind the world of their suffering and struggle. It was tremendously moving."

—A woman from Chesapeake, Virginia

"Very moving museum, painfully realistic, very extensive, quite impressed. History really comes to life."

—A woman from Hillsboro, Oregon

"This tour reaffirms that my duty as a U.S. Army officer is worthwhile and contributes to world peace."

—An officer from Chester, Virginia

Murray K. Carton of the Richmond area volunteers daily at the reception desk.

Dianna Gabay, graphic and fine artist, is Director of Exhibitions and Collections and is responsible for the outstanding quality of the museum exhibits.

Al Rosenbaum, retired businessman and sculptor who works in glass and metal, is museum Co-founder and Treasurer. Sylvia Rosenbaum volunteered to maintain financial records and handle all correspondence.

Mark E. Fetter, owner of Richmond Publishing and museum Co-founder and Secretary, approached Jay in 1997 about telling his story within a museum setting.

Jay M. Ipson, Co-founder, President, and Executive Director of the Virginia Holocaust Museum, is a Holocaust survivor of the Kovno ghetto/concentration camp.

Elly Ipson, secretary and treasurer of the former Ipson family-owned American Parts, now volunteers to maintain the museum database.

Exhibit Credits

All exhibitions designed by Dianna Gabay and Al Rosenbaum

Deportation—Mural artist Chris Kull

Wall of Honor—Dianna Gabay and Al Rosenbaum

Dachau/Buchenwald—Mannequins by Dianna Gabay; bunk bed, mannequin hands and
bowls by Thomas Kull; prisoner uniforms by Wolff Fording Company; gate by
Martin Rappa; mural artist Letitia Lee

Hyde Farmlands—Chickens by Dianna Gabay; mural by Janet Gilmore-Bryan's Virginia
Commonwealth University fall 2002 mural class

Kristallnacht—Dianna Gabay and Al Rosenbaum; mural artist Elizabeth Keller

St. Louis—Mural by Janet Gilmore's VCU summer 2002 mural class

Kovno Ghetto/Democratic Square—Mural artist Chris Kull; maps, mannequins, and
coal worker figures by Dianna Gabay; coal mural by Ian Wilkinson; Torah callig-
raphy by Michael R. McCauley

Paskovskis' Farm—Mural by Janet Gilmore's VCU spring 2003 mural class

Partisan—Mural artist Elizabeth Keller

Crematory oven cart—Martin Rappa

Liberation—Gate by Kenneth Olshansky, M.D.; mural by Janet Gilmore's VCU summer
2003 mural class

DP Camp—Mural artist Chris Kull

Exodus—Ship model by Howard Pinchefsky

Cyprus—Mural by Janet Gilmore's VCU spring 2003 mural class; tents by
Mark Rosenbaum

Palestine/Israel—Mural artist Chris Kull

Auditorium/Synagogue—Trademark Woodworking LLC (Marc Cohen); carvings by
Demetrios Art Studio (Demetrios Mavroudis, Ed.D.)

Cattle car—Alex Lebenstein, Jörg Richter, Tobias Brüggemann, Thomas Gottschewsky,
Erwin Kirschenbaum, Günter Meyer

Tower—Peninsula Glass Guild, designed by Beth G. Layne

Building architect—Jody Lahandra

Exhibition signage—Presentation Resources

Print matter—Keith Fabry

Steel work—Richmond Steel (Andy C. Jackson)

Carpenters—Mike Astrella, John Smith, Stuart Wilkinson

Other contributors—Captions/exhibit signage by Laura Henley and Molly Maffei; railroad
tracks by Michael R. McCauley

Special thanks to Barbara Hilow, Jessica Klein, Tom Kull, Terry Minter, Ashleigh Moody,
and Florian Oberleiter

Credits

Photographs—Dianna Gabay, Jay Ipson, Molly Maffei, and Brett Zwerdling

Photo compilation—Dianna Gabay

Captions—Molly Maffei

Bibliography

Bachrach, Susan D. 1994. *Tell Them We Remember: The Story of the Holocaust.* Boston:
Little, Brown and Company.

Gilbert, Martin. 1998. *Israel: A History.* New York: William Morrow and Company, Inc.

Landau, Ronnie S. 1992. *The Nazi Holocaust.* Chicago: Ivan R. Dee.

Rice Jr., Earle. 1998. *The Final Solution.* San Diego: Lucent Books, Inc.

ABOUT THE AUTHOR

Elisabeth Anne Custalow, a native of Richmond, Virginia, is a graduate of The College of William and Mary and is employed by the *Richmond Times-Dispatch*.

Index